THE ZENNED OUT GUIDE TO

UNDERSTANDING
THE WHEEL
OF THE YEAR

YOUR HANDBOOK TO HONORING THE
EIGHT SEASONAL CELEBRATIONS

CASSIE UHL

ROCK
POINT

INTRODUCTION

The Wheel of the Year is your call to come back to the rhythms of Mother Nature. In our not-so-distant past, we lived by nature. We grew our own food, stopped working when the sun went down, celebrated every solstice, and came together for support during cold winter months. Our modern lives have improved in many ways, but many of us have forgotten how close we're tied to nature. We no longer have to abide by the seasons, but that doesn't mean that we don't need to commune with Mother Earth.

Working with the seasons through the Wheel of the Year is a road map back home in many ways. Each seasonal celebration, or Sabbat, offers you moments to pause, reflect, and give thanks. I cannot think of better medicine for us as a species right now. This book is an illustrated guide to help you come back to the cyclical nature of Mother Earth and to honor where you came from— where we all came from.

WORKING WITH THE SEASONS WILL
BRING A SENSE OF GROUNDING TO YOUR
SPIRITUAL PRACTICE.

I invite you to make noticing and connecting with nature part of your daily routine as you read this book, and hopefully, even beyond this book. At the heart of each of these Sabbats is a deep reverence for nature. The Wheel of the Year in and of itself will align you with the earth, but you don't have to let it stop there. Try going for more regular walks, pay attention to what kinds of animals and blooms appear at different times of the year, and look for the lessons and beauty in each season (especially your least favorite ones!).

You do not have to identify as Wiccan, Pagan, or a witch to participate in the Wheel of the Year. The earth is for all of us. However, you might find, like I did, that these practices bring a sense of homecoming.

When I started my spiritual journey as a teenager, I was initially inspired by Eastern practices like yoga and Buddhism. I still enjoy these practices today but have since dedicated more time to learning about my personal lineage. When I was younger, I quickly understood that witchcraft, Wicca, and Paganism were deemed "bad" by many. There's still a strong stigma attached to these practices. Sadly, these stigmas kept me from exploring and better understanding my spiritual roots for many years.

My deeply spiritual grandmother came from England as a teenager, pregnant with my father. When I lost her in 2015, I began diving deeper into spiritual practices associated with ancient Celtic and Anglo-Saxon cultures in the United Kingdom.

I was pleasantly surprised to find how deeply I resonated with them. I realized so much of what I was already doing in my spiritual practice lined up with the nature-based spirituality of my cultural lineage. I also learned that the negative associations with witchcraft, Wicca, and Paganism were simply misinformed. At their heart, these practices are rooted in deep love and reverence for the natural world.

Today, my spiritual practice revolves around the Wheel of the Year, nature, and the change of seasons. The ebb and flow of the seasons remind me that no matter how technologically advanced we become as a species we are, and have always been, of the earth. Each seasonal sabbat is a cornerstone of my practice, a call to remember where I came from, and an opportunity to tune into the energy of the season.

The ways that I honor the Sabbats vary season to season, but meditation, my altars, and candle magick are consistent ways through which I bring meaning to the celebrations on the Wheel of the Year. If you ever shop at my little store, Zenned Out, in Gilbert, Arizona, you'll see my altar change with each season. I often share my store altar on social media, so you can still see it even if you're not local. In fact, the altar sections from each chapter of this book have been modeled after my store's seasonal altar!

I cannot think of a better healing salve for a world where so many of us are disconnected from the natural world than leaning into the wisdom of Mother Earth. Working with the Wheel of the Year has made me more whole and grounded in all areas of my life, and I know it can do the same for you too. Let's get started.

HOW TO USE THIS BOOK

You can read this book cover to cover or pick and choose different Sabbats to read about as they circle around. If you decide to pick and choose, I suggest reading the next chapter, so you have a strong understanding of the Wheel of the Year and where it comes from before diving into practice.

You might find it helpful to put up a picture of the Wheel of the Year with the dates of each Sabbat somewhere you'll see it regularly or buy a calendar that shows the dates of each Sabbat.

Each Sabbat chapter offers a variety of ways to connect with the season. You'll find in-depth correspondence lists for each season. Correspondences are energies that match or, as I like to say, "play nicely together." You'll also find a list of traditional rituals to honor each season. Lastly, you'll find various tools to connect with the energy of each season, like meditations, journal prompts, and card spreads to be used with tarot or oracle card decks.

I've found that connecting with the energy at the core of each season makes the Sabbats more accessible. For example, I focus more on the energy of gratitude and balance for the autumn equinox rather than the act of harvesting. For me, this expands the meaning of the Sabbats on the Wheel of the Year and makes them easier to work with from a modern standpoint. I include a section in each chapter to help you better understand the energy of each season and easy ways to connect to it through meditation and ritual.

CHAPTER I

THE WHEEL OF THE YEAR

We did not always have calendars to mark the passage of time, and time wasn't always viewed as being linear. We lived by the cycles of nature, the moon, the stars, and the sun. As we know it today, the Wheel of the Year is a relatively modern creation, but the practices associated with it are older than time. The eight Sabbats, or celebrations, on the wheel honor seasonal shifts and solar events that were integral to ancient people's lives.

··· ᑕ ᓚ ···

THE WHEEL OF THE YEAR BRINGS YOU BACK TO THE NATURAL CYCLES AND RHYTHMS OF THE EARTH.

··· ᓚ ᑐ ···

In this foundational chapter, you'll learn what you can expect to gain from working with the Wheel of the Year, what the Wheel of the Year is, and its history. I'll also help you understand some of the most common terms and labels often associated with the Wheel of the Year. When talking about Paganism, Wicca, and witchcraft, it can certainly feel a little confusing to know what's what. I get it! This chapter will give you everything you need to understand the basic terminology associated with the Wheel of the Year.

WHAT IS THE WHEEL
OF THE YEAR?

The Wheel of the Year is a collection of eight Sabbats evenly spaced throughout the year based on nature and the sun's movement. The eight Sabbats can be broken down into four solar events and four seasonal shifts. See the illustrations on pages 12 to 13 for how these celebrations appear on the Wheel of the Year.

The four solar events are the winter solstice, spring equinox, summer solstice, and autumn equinox. These solar events are often referred to as "quarter days" or "lesser-Sabbats." The four seasonal shifts happen between each of the solar events and signal a seasonal change or an important harvest season. The four seasonal shifts are called Imbolc, Beltane, Lughnasadh, and Samhain. These celebrations are often referred to as "cross-quarter days" or "fire festivals." The sets of four celebrations interlock to create the eight celebrations on the Wheel.

You will likely come across information and people using a variety of names for each of the Sabbats. For example, Lughnasadh is often referred to as Lammas. Many people who work with the Wheel of the Year choose not to use the given names for the quarter-day celebrations and simply refer to them as the solstice or equinox. We'll explore the reasons for this in the history section coming up. I'll also go into more detail about the name origins of each season in their respective chapters.

The eight Sabbats fall on similar days each year but can vary slightly depending on each calendar year, where you live, and your personal preferences. Because the four seasonal shifts are based on your natural surroundings, you might find dates near the suggested Sabbats that make more sense to you. Even within our relative hemispheres, the seasons and temperatures vary dramatically. For example, I live in the hot and dry climate of Arizona. I know that the floral oleander and magenta bougainvillea come into full bloom at Beltane. It's a signal to me to prepare to honor the season. For those living in the southern hemisphere, you'll likely want to use the opposite dates to honor each Sabbat. However, if you prefer to celebrate the Sabbats on the same dates as the northern hemisphere, that's okay too!

You may begin to notice signs from nature around you as well. When you do, you may feel called to celebrate the seasons when you see these shifts, rather than by the dates in this book. Not only is this okay, but it's encouraged! Working with the Wheel of the Year is a personal practice because it's based on our relationship with nature.

Now that you have a firm understanding of the Wheel of the Year, let's start to understand some of its patchwork of history.

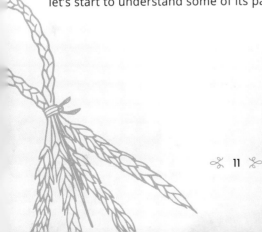

THE WHEEL OF THE YEAR

NORTHERN HEMISPHERE

THE WHEEL OF THE YEAR

SOUTHERN HEMISPHERE

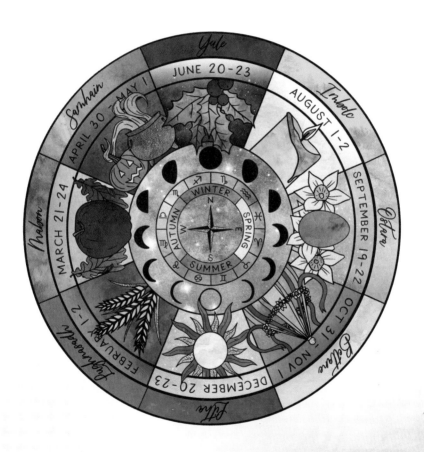

HISTORY OF THE
WHEEL OF THE YEAR

The Wheel of the Year stems from various celebrations from ancient Celtic, Anglo-Saxon, and Germanic cultures. There's actually no historical evidence that any one culture celebrated all eight Sabbats as they're known today. Rather, the Wheel of the Year is a beautiful consolidation of the most common seasonal and solar celebrations from various cultures in what we now call northern and western Europe. I'd also like to point out that you don't need to have ancestry in Northern or Western Europe to work with the Wheel of the Year. In fact, many cultures around the world work with the seasons. The Wheel acts as a portal for all to work alongside nature in deep and meaningful ways.

Before Christianity dominated northern and western Europe, there were, and still are, rich and deeply spiritual practices. The reverence for nature associated with the Wheel of the Year is rooted in these very practices. Though often given the blanket label of Pagan, many of these spiritual practices go back to the Druids, Awen, and ancient shamans of the region. Minimal written history is available because most of these old ways were passed down orally. Regardless of written history, it's easy to see the importance of the solar celebrations to cultures in these areas. Impressive structures still remain, like Stonehenge in England and Newgrange in Ireland, that tell a story of being very well connected to nature and our sun's movement.

When Christianity began to take over, many of these oral traditions were lost, often by force. The loss of wisdom from the attempted erasure of these spiritual traditions may never be fully known. If you know or suspect that you have ancestry in these areas, then working with the seasons through the Wheel of the Year is a powerful way to reclaim your spiritual roots. Furthermore, it grants you the opportunity to heal deep ancestral wounds associated with the attempted eradication of the old ways of living in alignment with the earth.

As we know it today, the Wheel of the Year was a collaboration that took place in the mid-twentieth century between a handful of Neo-Pagans and Wiccans. The most notable and influential people to have a hand in creating the Wheel of the Year were Gerald Gardner, also known as the "Father of Wicca;" Ross Nichols, the founder of the Order of Bards, Ovates, Druids; and Aidan Kelly. This was when the four solar celebrations and four cross-quarter celebrations were combined into a unified system that we know today as the Wheel of the Year.

The names of each celebration, for the most part, stem from either Celtic or Anglo-Saxon cultures. Though some names do align with ancient celebrations, not all of them do. For example, the name often used for the autumn equinox, Mabon, was only coined by Aidan Kelly in the 1970s based on a Welsh mythological figure. There are other common names, like Lammas, that are Christianized versions of the original Sabbats.

Though the Wheel of the Year's design and the names of some of the celebrations were birthed more recently, the inception of honoring the cyclical nature of the seasons is far from modern. The Wheel of the Year simply offers a concise and simple template to work with the seasons. You can choose to use the names of the celebrations as I outline them here or use others. It is the act of working alongside nature that is at the heart of the Wheel of the Year, not the names we assign to each phase.

At this point, your head might be spinning with different terms like Pagan, witch, Wicca, and Druid. I get it! When I started my journey working with the Wheel of the Year, I found it brought up more questions than answers. I also didn't know what to call myself. If you're wondering where you fit in or what to call yourself, I made a short list of common labels associated with those who work with the Wheel of the Year. If none of these fit, that's okay. You do not need to assign a label to yourself to work with the Wheel of the Year. But, if one of these terms does interest you, you'll have a better idea of where to look next!

The truth is, we may never know the extent to which these ancient peoples honored the celebrations on the Wheel of the Year. What we do know is that the seasonal shifts, the sun, nature, and the growing seasons were of utmost importance to them and their livelihood. Even though our modern take of working with the seasons through the Wheel of the Year likely differs from exactly what our ancestors practiced, it is still a valuable and meaningful tool to live in closer alignment with their ways.

KEY TERMS

- **Paganism**: An umbrella term for those who do not practice the most common religions and who honor many different gods and goddesses or nature.

- **Neo-Paganism**: A modern reclamation of pre-Christian Pagan practices.

- **Wicca**: Modern Pagan religion started in the mid-twentieth century that worships nature.

- **Witch**: Someone who practices spellwork and magick.

- **Druidry**: The ancient spiritual practices honored by various indigenous peoples of northern Europe.

CHAPTER 2

HOW TO WORK WITH THE WHEEL OF THE YEAR

f there's one thing I'd like you to hold close to your heart as you work with the Wheel of the Year, it's that your practice will be unique to you. You can't mess up working alongside nature. There's no candle color you can burn that will ruin your seasonal celebration. The natural world that you live amidst and your relationship to nature are extremely personal. Therefore, your practice will be, too.

SCULPT A PATH THAT WORKS FOR YOU.

The suggestions I share throughout this book are intended to be a starting place for you. I encourage you to build on what's outlined in these chapters and create your own rituals and celebrations as you become more familiar with your area's natural cycles. As we already discussed, the Wheel of the Year itself is a rather modern creation, so there's no need to be strict with how you honor each seasonal celebration. I also want you to know that you don't need to work with the Wheel in all of these ways. Your seasonal practice can be as simple or as complex as you want it to be.

In this chapter, you'll learn some of the ways to work with the Wheel of the Year, what you'll need to get started, and how to weave what you learn into your everyday life.

SOLITARY VS. SOCIAL PRACTICE

The primary differentiation in your practice will be whether you decide to make your practice solitary or with others, often called a coven. Of course, this doesn't have to be a decision you make right now, and it's okay to change it up and practice solitary with a sprinkling of social celebrations, or vice versa. The reason I point this out is that for many, a solitary practice may be your only option, and I want you to know that's okay.

Hedge witchcraft is a solitary practice that leans heavily on working alongside nature. Hedge witches often work with herbs and plant magick. In the past, witches who practiced in this way often lived on the outskirts of town, hence the term *hedge*. If the Wheel of the Year and a solo practice are appealing to you, I suggest exploring hedge witchery as well!

If you live in a small community, there may not be other witches or Pagans around who want to have bonfires for each fire festival. Not participating in some of the most common practices for each season, which often included social activities like bonfires and meals, does not make your practice less powerful.

If you wish to celebrate the seasons with others, metaphysical supply stores that specialize in witchcraft will often hold seasonal celebrations or classes in line with the Wheel of the Year. If you can't find any such local shops that offer seasonal celebrations, starting your own group, either online or in person, is also a perfectly viable option!

HONORING YOUR
LOCAL SEASONALITY

Climate change and your local seasonality will undoubtedly affect how you work with the Wheel of the Year. It's entirely possible, and quite likely, that the timing of the seasons where you live will vary from the exact dates offered in this book. Of course, the four solar festivals (Ostara, Litha, Mabon, and Yule) will occur at the same time regardless, but when you decide to honor each Sabbat is truly up to you.

Our ancestors relied heavily on local seasonality to honor the Sabbats. For example, it was common practice to rely on signs from nature rather than specific dates for the cross-quarter festivals (Imbolc, Beltane, Lughnasadh, and Samhain.) I encourage you to do the same and look for changes in your environment that line up with the Sabbats on the Wheel of the Year.

This is your practice, so don't hesitate to make it your own! For example, there are times when I set up my seasonal altars early due to the climate where I live. It's not uncommon for me to feel inspired to set up my seasonal altar for Ostara before the actual equinox. The varieties of climates aren't reasons not to work with the Wheel; rather, they are opportunities to connect more deeply with the world around you.

SUGGESTED TOOLS

At the most basic level, all you *really* need to work with the Wheel of the Year is a desire to connect with nature. If you live in a lush natural environment, this will be easy. If you live in an urban area, this is a great time to do some research to discover local parks and nature trails in your locale. However, don't let not living near a lush forest stop you from connecting with nature daily.

What you'll need:

♦ Journal or book of shadows

♦ Altar space(s)

♦ Items from nature for each season

A book of shadows, also called a grimoire, is a collection of personal magickal notes, spells, and recipes. This is a term coined by Gerald Gardner, the founder of Wicca, in the 1950s. You can call your journal a book of shadows, a grimoire, or simply a journal.

Working with a journal will be helpful as you work with the seasons. A dedicated journal will give you a place to record notes about what's going on in your environment for each season. As you continue to work with the seasons, you'll likely want to record your rituals, recipes, and spells to refer back to. Personally, I'm not great at journaling regularly, so I'm not going to tell you that you need to journal every day to have a meaningful practice.

I do like to write down my most treasured spells, rituals, and recipes for future reference. Find a journaling schedule that works for you!

Think of your altar as a tool to invite the energy of each season into your home. Altars are also a great place to honor nature, practice rituals and spells, and connect with your ancestors. In my opinion, altars are an integral part of working with the Wheel of the Year. Altars have always been a part of my practice, so you will see an emphasis on working with them in this book.

Your altar can be as simple or as complex as you want it to be. Altars can be inside and outside, and you can have more than one (in fact, I suggest having more than one!). If working with an altar is new to you, I recommend starting small. Check out the steps on pages 24 to 25 to create an altar for your current season.

HOW TO CREATE AN ALTAR

1. Select a space in your home that you'll be able to connect with regularly. This can be as simple as a windowsill above your sink or a special shelf that you purchase.

2. Clean your altar space physically.

3. Clean your altar space energetically with incense smoke, smoke from dried herbs, a bell, or your energy.

4. Select items that correspond with your current season. These could be items from the natural world (taken responsibly and ethically, of course), items from your home, handmade items, or purchased items.

5. As you place each item on your altar, do so with the intention of deep respect and honor for the natural world. If you work with any goddesses or gods, this is a great time to call on them to join you as you place each item. Alternatively, you can call in the energy of the four elements.

6. Place the items intuitively in a way that feels good to you.

7. Connect with your altar daily. This is a great place to write in your journal, perform rituals, or create a daily meditation practice.

8. As a show of gratitude, keep your altar clean and fresh. Replace items that wilt or go stale. Clean your altar physically and energetically anytime it starts to collect dust.

9. Refresh your altar for each Sabbat or when you feel called to.

DIFFERENT KINDS OF SEASONAL RITUALS

Some of the suggested rituals in this book are traditional, and others are not. As I've mentioned, I like to connect with the energy of each season, and you'll find that reflected in many of my ritual suggestions. The ways you choose to honor each season will depend on your personal practice, the season itself, where you live, and how much time you have during a given season.

If you never celebrate around a bonfire, you can still work with the Wheel of the Year. I promise, there's no "witch scorecard" waiting for you at the end of each season! Allow your practice to wax, wane, and evolve in its own unique way. Check out the next page for some of the most common ways to honor each Sabbat. I'll share more specific ways to honor each Sabbat in the coming chapters, but this gives you an idea of how varied working with the Wheel of the Year can be.

There will likely be some Sabbats you resonate with more than others. For this reason, you will probably do more for some Sabbats and less for others. This is not only normal but encouraged! It's important to build rituals into your seasonal celebrations that resonate with you rather than doing what you think you should for each season. Even though social media makes it seem like working with the Wheel of the Year is more about checking things off a list, it's actually about connecting with nature and the season's energy.

WAYS TO WORK WITH THE
WHEEL OF THE YEAR

MEDITATION

PLANTING, GROWING,
& HARVESTING

JOURNALING

HONORING
SPECIFIC GODS
& GODDESSES

SPELLWORK
& MAGICK

SEASONAL
RITUALS &
CELEBRATING
WITH OTHERS

ALTARS

SPECIAL FOODS
& RECIPES

BEING IN
NATURE

LIVING CYCLICALLY

Working with the Wheel of the Year teaches you how to live in flow with life cycles. Everything about us and the natural world is cyclical, yet so much of our human thinking, and how we work, has been trained to be linear. Can you imagine how much more balanced and whole we would be as a society if we lived more cyclically? The dormant seasons in nature show us that periods of rest are not only nice but also necessary. The interconnected root systems of trees show us how to care for one another when needed.

LIVING CYCLICALLY CREATES SPACE FOR PERIODS OF ACTIVITY AND PERIODS OF REST.

The Wheel of the Year will help you live more cyclically and understand other cycles of life on a deeper level, which, I believe, will not only spark healing within yourself but will trickle out to others as well. In the following pages, I'll outline various ways to work with some of the cycles that correspond with the Wheel of the Year, including lunar phases, the story of the god and goddess, the passage of time, and life and death.

◁◡ LUNAR PHASES ◡▷

In each of the chapters about the eight Sabbats, you'll notice that I include a section about its corresponding moon phase. This is because the celebrations on the Wheel of the Year perfectly mirror the phases of the moon. In my practice, the moon goes through nine primary phases. The ninth phase is the dark moon (the phase right before the new moon).

Some people who work with the moon include the dark moon phase; others do not. Because I do work with the dark moon, I combine the dark and new moon phase for Yule. The energy associated with each moon phase and Sabbat aligns as well. Take a look at page 31 to learn more about the moon phases.

The moon affects the flow of water and is therefore uniquely intertwined with nature. When you marry your understanding of the lunar phases with the natural world, you'll gain a greater appreciation for the cyclical nature of life. The seasons, day to day, may seem to stretch on forever, especially during the cold winter months, but the much shorter lunar cycle reminds us that all phases are temporary.

You can also find ways to combine the lunar phases' energy with the seasonal celebrations of the Wheel of the Year. For example, a full moon near or at the time of the summer solstice is extra potent because it is the peak of energy for the sun and the moon. It certainly isn't necessary to notice or work with all of these layered energies, but it will likely become second nature as you tune yourself to more cyclical living.

ESBATS

Esbats are celebrations or meetings that occur on full moons in between the seasonal Sabbats. The moon was a great timekeeper for our ancestors, and full moons were an ideal way to track the passage of time. It's been common practice in various cultures to name the full moons according to what season they fall in, to use them as seasonal markers. Full moons are an ideal time to practice magick of all kinds and honor the season.

PHASES OF THE MOON

NEW
MOON
Hope, openness,
rebirth

WAXING
CRESCENT
Declarations,
options, fertile
ground

FIRST
QUARTER
Focus, growth,
motivation

WAXING
GIBBOUS
Momentum,
adaptation,
transformation

FULL
MOON
Expansion,
power, magick

WANING
GIBBOUS
Reflection,
receiving,
contemplation

LAST
QUARTER
Surrender,
allowing, letting go

WANING
CRESCENT
Endings, evolution,
acceptance

DARK
MOON
Integration, rest,
introspection

For some ancient peoples and practicing Wiccans and Neo-Druids, the Wheel of the Year tells a story of the god and goddess.

Though there are specific gods and goddesses associated with many of the Sabbats, they vary from culture to culture, so for this section, I will simply refer to them as the god and goddess. If you feel called to work with associated deities of the season, this section will offer a deeper understanding of their role in each Sabbat.

THE TRIPLE GODDESS

The Triple Goddess represents the three stages of the goddess: maiden, mother, and crone. These energies are represented, respectively, as the waxing moon, full moon, and waning moon phases. We can also see these energies represented in the ever-changing seasons on the Wheel of the Year. The maiden is associated with fertile springtime. The mother is associated with the fullness of summer and the harvest season. The wise crone is associated with the darkness and rest associated with the wintertime. It is also important to note that the goddess never dies, she is always present simply in different phases.

The god and goddess perform a dance of sorts each year that is played out by the earth's changing seasons. This is a way for the seasons to tell a story and humanize their cyclical nature. Marrying the cycles of the earth with the story of the god and goddess is a poetic reminder that you can find the same cycles within yourself. You and the earth are one in the same, always connected, and permanently intertwined.

The narrative of the god and goddess can vary from person to person. If this narrative interests you there are many, more detailed, stories you can explore for each season, but here's a short synopsis of how the story of the god and goddess plays out each cycle:

·•◊ SAMHAIN ◊•·

At Samhain, the goddess is in her crone phase, and retreats within to alchemize and transform for the cycle ahead. The god is dormant within her.

·•◊ YULE ◊•·

The god is reborn with the returning light of the sun as the days slowly increase in light.

·•◊ IMBOLC ◊•·

The goddess begins to awaken into the maiden phase and can be seen as small signs of life beginning to awaken in the natural world.

·•◐ OSTARA ◑•·

The goddess fully embodies her maiden aspect as nature begins to emerge from the cold winter. It is at this point that the god enters the scene again, captivated by the maiden.

·•◐ BELTANE ◑•·

The goddess is at her most fertile time, and she and the god form a sacred union.

·•◐ LITHA ◑•·

The warmth and duration of the sun signifies that the god is at his peak of power. The god and the goddess marry.

·•◐ LUGHNASADH ◑•·

The goddess embodies her mother phase, ready to rule without the god. The energy of the god is given to the crops.

·•◐ MABON ◑•·

The god retreats into the forest and acts as a protector of the plants and animals. The goddess begins to retreat within, mourning the loss of the god.

For many of our ancestors, time was not viewed as something linear. The seasons of nature were their only framework of time, and the seasons were cyclical, so it makes sense that our ancestors would view themselves as part of that same cycle. Every ending naturally indicates a new beginning. Working with the Wheel of the Year is an invitation to view both time and death from a new perspective.

Death and loss were not the ends, only an opportunity to be repurposed or reborn anew. Rather than striving for an end, we can view each phase as an important part of a never-ending cycle. You cannot work with the Wheel of the Year and seasons and not confront death. Death is part of the natural cycle of life, and therefore not something to be feared.

This isn't to say that death and loss cannot be difficult, but for our ancestors and for many practicing this path, death is not final. It is simply a part of a larger cycle. Death, decomposition, and phases of inaction are important and necessary parts of the Wheel of the Year. The reframing of time and death will happen naturally as you continue to align yourself with nature. This wisdom is not something to be forced but is a gift you'll come to understand with each passing season.

With these suggestions in mind, it's time to embark on your journey through each seasonal celebration on the Wheel of the Year. Your journey begins with Samhain.

CHAPTER 3

SAMHAIN

THE VEIL IS THIN. IT'S TIME
TO CONNECT WITHIN.

The most sacred and treasured of all the Sabbats for most witches and Pagans, Samhain (pronounced sau-win or so-wen) is considered the witch's New Year. Samhain is one of four cross-quarter, or fire, festivals, which falls between the autumn equinox and the winter solstice. It is honored on October 31 in the northern hemisphere and on April 30 in the southern hemisphere.

The overlap of Samhain and Halloween is no coincidence. Halloween dates right back to the Celts with Samhain. Over time, Samhain was molded by Christianity to be a time to fear the dead rather than venerate our ancestors. Because Samhain is such a sacred and important Sabbat, it found a way to work itself into our modern celebrations through Halloween.

Practically speaking, our ancestors viewed Samhain as the third and final festival of the harvest. It marks the official end of summer and denotes a time to take shelter with family and prepare for winter. Final harvests are made, and animals are taken to slaughter in preparation for colder months. The season of Samhain is the final push in anticipation of harsh winters on the way. During this time, the goddess of the earth is in her crone phase, retreating to rest and transform anew.

Energetically, Samhain is designated as a unique time to honor and connect with our ancestors who have passed on as well as otherworldly realms. The veil between the spirit world and the physical world is at its thinnest on October 31. The spirits of our ancestors and fae folk are said to walk among us during this time. Due to the thin veil between worlds, it is common to practice divination, magick, and protection rituals during Samhain.

CONNECT WITH AND HONOR THOSE WHO'VE COME BEFORE YOU.

This season corresponds to the crone, or wise woman archetype, and death. The earth has gone through its growth phase (the maiden) and production and fruition phase (the mother), and now it is time to retreat within to rest for a new cycle. Death is an integral part of any natural phase. As you'll learn from working with the Wheel of the Year, death is not something to be feared. Insd, it is the forebearer to new growth. It is within this deep and reflective incubation period that we begin our seasonal wheel.

·◦◊ TIP ◊◦·

The thin veil offers a unique opportunity to welcome, honor, and connect with those on the other side as if they were here to visit. Photographs, treasured items, favorite foods of the departed loved one, or a candle would each make a beautiful offering during this time.

SAMHAIN CORRESPONDENCES

·•◊ THEMES ◊•·
Ancestral connections, releasing, cleansing, death,
divination, protection, the underworld

·•◊ MOON PHASE ◊•·
Waning crescent

·•◊ CRYSTALS ◊•·
Amethyst, labradorite, obsidian, onyx, hematite

·•◊ COLORS ◊•·
Purple, black, silver, orange

·•◊ TOOLS & SPECIAL ITEMS ◊•·
Besom (broom), cauldron, salt,
divination tools (pendulum, tarot cards, scrying mirror)

·•◊ PLANTS & SCENTS ◊•·
Mugwort, cinnamon, clove, patchouli, mullein, garlic

·•◊ FOODS ◊•·
Apples, pomegranate, pumpkin, squash, nuts, seeds, meat

·•◊ RUNES ◊•·
Algiz, Ansuz, Perthro, Othala, Isa

·•◊ ZODIAC ◊•·
Scorpio

·•◊ GODS AND GODDESSES ◊•·
Arawn, Cernunnos, Gwyn ap Nudd, Herne, Odin, Loki, Hades, Cailleach,
Cerridwen, Hecate, Lilith, Persephone, Inanna, Ishtar, Baba Yaga, Rhiannon

SAMHAIN ALTAR

CONNECTING WITH THE ENERGY OF SAMHAIN

The energy of Samhain invites you to connect with deep wisdom within yourself, your ancestors, and the spirit world. This season is an exploratory call inward. Two of the best ways to connect with the energy of Samhain is through divination practices, connecting with spirits on the other side, and honoring your ancestors in spirit. Divination is the act of opening yourself up to psychic information. I prefer to view psychic work as information from spirit to help me grow into a better version of myself, rather than "telling the future."

YOUR CRUMBLING ALLOWS YOUR REBIRTH. ALLOW YOURSELF TO FALL APART.

Samhain is also viewed as an important time to perform shadow work. Shadow work is the act of making a conscious effort to explore and understand aspects of yourself that are often ignored, like fear, shame, and sadness. Shadow work can bring up uncomfortable feelings; however, the Triple Goddess's crone aspect understands the importance of facing all parts of ourselves, even the challenging ones. Use the following journal prompts, card spread, and meditation to explore challenging aspects of your personality and soul and to make room for new growth in the coming cycles.

SAMHAIN AND THE WANING CRESCENT MOON PHASE

The waning moon phase is associated with releasing, letting go, and acceptance of what is. It's a time to fully embody the wise woman aspect of the Triple Goddess. The waning moon phase's energy understands that life isn't rainbows all the time and that the shadow side of life holds deep wisdom.

SAMHAIN JOURNAL REFLECTIONS

Use these journal prompts to help you explore your shadow side and connect with your ancestors during Samhain.

- ♦ What areas of my life have I been avoiding?

- ♦ Why do I fear looking at these areas of my life?

- ♦ What is my relationship with death and dying?

- ♦ What is my relationship like with my ancestral heritage?

- ♦ How can I cultivate a deeper relationship with my ancestors?

SAMHAIN CARD SPREAD

This five-card spread is intended to help you identify parts of your life that are ready to be transformed, connect with your inner crone, and receive a message from your ancestors. Perform this card spread with your favorite oracle or tarot card deck.

1. What areas of my life need to transform or die away?

2. How can I best grieve these parts of myself and my life?

3. In what areas of my life do I need to embody the wise woman?

4. Where do I need more protection in my life?

5. What message do my ancestors have for me?

RITUALS FOR SAMHAIN

Rituals for Samhain revolve around death, intuition, and ancestral connection. Here's a list of common traditional rituals associated with the season of Samhain, as well as a more in-depth ritual to help you protect your space during this season.

♦ Honor loved ones passed on.

♦ Give offerings to your ancestors.

♦ Connect with the crone archetype.

♦ Hold a "mute" or "silent" supper.

♦ Practice divination with a tool of your choice.

♦ Explore shadow work.

♦ Make a besom (or broom).

♦ Carve a jack-o'-lantern.

♦ Cleanse the energy of your home.

SAMHAIN MEDITATION FOR SPIRITUAL CONNECTION

For this meditation, you'll connect to your third eye, also known as the seat of intuition, to help inspire a connection to the spirit world. Set aside 15 to 30 minutes to perform this meditation. If you'd like to hold some crystals in your hands during this meditation, amethyst and labradorite are great options.

1. Take a comfortable seat, close your eyes, start to pay attention to your breath, and become more aware of your physical body.

2. Begin to send your breath into your low belly, then extend the length of each inhale and exhale.

3. Continue to remain aware of your breath but draw your attention to your third eye (the area between your brow bones).

4. Visualize a deep purple light glowing around your third eye. Imagine that this light grows brighter and larger with each breath that you take.

5. Continue to focus on your breath and visualize the purple light growing until it completely envelops your body.

6. Notice how it feels in your body to open your intuition.

7. Ask aloud or in your mind for any spirits, ancestors, or guides with your highest good in mind to give you a sign. Pay attention to new sensations in your body, visualizations that appear in your mind's eye, or thoughts that seem to come from out of nowhere. If working with the spirit world is new to you, signs could be extremely subtle.

8. At this point, you can decide to continue connecting with the spirit realm or retreat back to the physical realm.

9. When you choose to come out of the meditation, thank any guides, spirits, or ancestors for connecting with you.

10. Visualize the purple light retreating back into your third eye.

11. Come back to focusing on your breath, become more aware of your physical body, and open your eyes.

PROTECTION RITUAL FOR YOUR HOME

Because the veil between the spirit world and the physical world is so thin during Samhain, protection magick is an ideal practice. It's a good idea to get in the habit of giving your living space some energetic protection around this time of year. Here is how you can protect your space from unwanted energies.

You'll need:

♦ Cleansing and protective smoke of choice, like dried mugwort, rosemary, cedar, or incense

♦ A fireproof dish for burning your herbs, like a cauldron or tray for your incense

♦ Matches or lighter

♦ A white candle

♦ A fireproof dish for your candle

- ♦ Salt

- ♦ Water

- ♦ A bowl

- ♦ 4 pieces of black tourmaline

Steps:

1. Begin your home protection ritual by calling on any guides, spirits, or ancestors you work with to assist you.

2. Smoke cleanse your space, using incense or dried herbs of choice. As you cleanse, visualize any negative energies leaving your space.

3. Light your white candle and walk around every corner of your space, inviting in the energy of a higher power, god, or goddess you work with. When you're done, set the white candle on your stove (the modern-day hearth) to burn as you complete your ritual. *Note*: Never leave your candle unattended.

4. Put salt and water in your bowl and mix them together.

·•◊ TIP ◊•·

Put your saltwater in a spray bottle for easy application!

5. Sprinkle the saltwater around the perimeter of your home, paying particular attention to doorways and windows. Salt is a protective and shielding tool and will help keep negative energy from reentering your space.

6. Place one of the black tourmaline stones in each of the four corners of your home.

·•◊ TIP ◊•·

For long-term protection, you can bury the black tourmaline stones outside your home, right outside each corner.

7. Return to your white candle. Repeat this phrase, or something like it, aloud or in your head, "Only allow energy in this space with my highest and best good in mind. I am safe and protected, always. So it is."

8. Let your candle burn fully. If you're unable to let your candle burn completely, snuff it out with a candle snuffer rather than blowing it out. *Note*: Always use proper fire safety and care when working with candles. Never leave your candle unattended.

9. Thank any guides, spirits, or ancestors for assisting you in your protection ritual.

CHAPTER 4

YULE

REST IN THE DARKNESS.
THE LIGHT OF A NEW
SEASON IS COMING.

We begin our seasonal wheel with the Sabbat of Yule and the winter solstice. This time marks the shortest day of the year and an important tipping point when the days will slowly become longer. This season is the dark night before the dawn that ushers in the sense of hope and new beginnings. In the northern hemisphere, Yule is celebrated on December 21 or 22 and on June 20 or 21 in the southern hemisphere.

The winter solstice is an important time for cultures around the world. Sacred sites that line up with the rising solstice sun can be found far beyond Stonehenge. Though we are still very much reliant on the sun for modern life, our ancestors relied upon the sun even more so. Its return was of utmost importance. The return of longer days brought by the winter solstice sparked a sense of hope in our ancestors that we may never fully understand in these modern times. This shift into lighter days was a time to celebrate. Family and friends would come together during this season to find strength and warmth through the harsh winter and honor the return of the light.

During Yule, there are still many dark and cold weeks of winter ahead. The darkness associated with Yule is a call to reflect on and honor everything that transpired in the previous year. The call inward asks you to acknowledge difficulties that may have occurred so you can pull them in and heal them, only to be transformed into a more whole being. This season asks you to hold space for both the darkness and the light and to see the value in both. Though Yule can be a celebratory time, it is also a deeply reflective time, especially for solitary practitioners.

YULE CORRESPONDENCES

THEMES
Duality, reflection, rest, hope, new beginnings, transformations, gratitude

MOON PHASE
Dark and new moon

ELEMENT
Earth

CRYSTALS
Bloodstone, garnet, malachite, snowflake obsidian, smoky quartz

COLORS
Green, red, white, gold, silver

TOOLS & SPECIAL ITEMS
Candles, Yule log

PLANTS & SCENTS
Cedar, juniper, pine, holly, fir, mistletoe, oak, birch, frankincense, myrrh

FOODS
Nuts, seeds, root vegetables, meat, wassail, spiced cakes

RUNES
Dagaz, Isa, Perth

ZODIAC
Sagittarius, Capricorn

GODS AND GODDESSES
Baldur, Holly King, Saturn, Mithras, Odin, Cailleach, Holle, Frigga, Demeter

YULE ALTAR

CONNECTING WITH THE ENERGY OF YULE

The energy of Yule provides an opportunity for deep rest and reflection. The energy of this season is very passive. Passive activities at this time may include solitary creative projects, reading, restorative meditations, enjoying and tending to your physical needs, and reflective journaling. Though this is a tIme when many of us join together to celebrate with family, this season's overarching energy is one of restoration and solitude. Much of nature is dormant during this time, so it is a call for you to retreat within as well.

WHEN YOU MAKE SPACE FOR REST AND INTEGRATION, YOU HONOR YOUR WHOLE SPIRIT.

·•◌ TIP ◌•·

Actively seek out ways to bring more rest into your life during this season. Consider creating a nightly or weekly ritual of drinking a soothing tea, taking a bath, or journaling to ensure you're giving yourself enough time and space to reflect on the previous year.

The energy associated with the New Year, which falls very near to Yule, often brings a desire to make big changes and take on new projects. Rather than jumping into action, Yule invites a sense of openness and curiosity about different directions you could take in the year ahead. Instead of making bold resolutions, I invite you to open yourself up to spirit for how to navigate the year. Often, our egos may get in the way of a path that's actually in better alignment or even better than what we originally thought. The energy of this season invites a sense of exploring all possibilities with inquisitiveness. Use the following journal prompts, card spread, and meditation to honor rest and inspire a sense of curiosity about your year ahead.

··· ⌒ ···

THE LIGHT OF A NEW SEASON IS
COMING. ALLOW YOURSELF TO
FEEL HOPE FOR THE UNSEEN.

··· ⌒ ···

YULE AND THE DARK MOON
AND NEW MOON

The moon phase correspondences for this season are both the dark and the new moon. The dark moon is an important lunar phase often left out. It happens when the moon is completely invisible in the night sky and comes right before the new moon. The dark moon is an important time in the lunar cycle that calls for deep rest and integration. The proceeding new moon welcomes the return of light and hope.

Though it is not the time to take action or plant new seeds (physically or metaphorically), it is a time to be open to new possibilities. There is a deep sense of duality present in the essence of this season.

YULE JOURNAL REFLECTIONS

Use these journal prompts to help you reflect on the previous year and find gratitude for where you're at now.

- ◆ What are some of the most difficult experiences or hardships I've experienced over the previous year?

- ◆ How have these experiences shaped me currently?

- ◆ Have I been able to see any growth, learning opportunities, or even gratitude from these experiences?

- ◆ What is my relationship with rest? Do I rest enough? How would my life look if I allowed myself to rest more?

- ◆ What new possibilities or paths do I feel a sense of curiosity or hope about in the year ahead?

YULE CARD SPREAD

This six-card spread is intended to help you clarify what areas of your life need further integration and rest. It will also help you find more gratitude and open yourself up to new possibilities. Perform this card spread with your favorite oracle or tarot card deck.

1. What is there to learn from the lessons I experienced over the last year?

2. In what areas of my emotional life do I need more integration or care?

3. In what areas of my spiritual life do I need more integration or care?

4. How can I bring more healing and rest to my physical body?

5. Where can I find more gratitude in my life?

6. Where in my life are new paths or opportunities available to me?

RITUALS FOR YULE

To celebrate this season's energy, rituals revolve around resting, reflecting, gratitude, and celebrating the return of the sun. Here's a list of common rituals associated with Yule and the winter solstice season and a couple of more elaborate rituals to try.

- ♦ Make a Yule log.

- ♦ Decorate a Yule tree.

- ♦ Enjoy spiced warm cider called wassail.

- ♦ Give gifts.

- ♦ Connect with your family or chosen family.

- ♦ Light candles to honor the return of the sun.

- ♦ Rest and reflect on the previous year.

YULE RESTORATIVE MEDITATION

For this meditation, you'll focus on accessing deep rest, allowing your mind and body time to integrate. Set aside 20 to 30 minutes to perform this meditation. If you'd like to hold some crystals in your hands or place some on your body during this meditation, smoky quartz, bloodstone, or garnet are all great options. You may fall asleep during this meditation. Consider setting an alarm if you need to end the meditation at a certain time.

1. Lay down in a bed or on the floor and make yourself as comfortable as possible. If you'd like, you can place some pillows under your legs to take the pressure off your back.

2. Quiet your mind and become aware of your breath.

3. Start sending each inhale deep into your belly.

4. Begin extending your inhales and your exhales.

5. Become more aware of your body. Notice where your body feels good and where it feels achy.

6. Starting at your toes, say, "I feel my toes," then visualize sending your breath into that part of your body.

7. Repeat step 6 for every part of your body, slowly working your way up from your toes to the crown of your head. Don't rush it. Listen to each part of your body as you tune in to it and send it energy from your breath.

8. If thoughts come up for specific body parts, notice them and ask whether anything needs to be resolved in that area. If feelings arise as this happens, allow your emotions to come and go as they need.

9. If you fall asleep before you get to the crown of your head, that's okay. If you make it to the crown of your head, you can rest there for as long as you'd like or go to sleep.

10. If you decide to get up from your meditation, do so slowly by rolling over onto your side in the fetal position before slowly getting up.

LETTING GO GRATITUDE RITUAL

Yule is a time to reflect on everything that happened in the previous year, both positive and negative. The darkness of Yule is an opportunity to process difficult situations that have gone untended to help heal them and find gratitude for the abundance you do have.

You'll need:

- ◆ 2 pieces of paper
- ◆ Pen or pencil
- ◆ Snowflake obsidian and malachite (optional)
- ◆ Matches or a lighter
- ◆ A fireproof dish like a cauldron

Steps:

1. Collect your items and ensure you have 15 to 30 minutes of quiet time.

2. Take 1 to 2 minutes to ground and center yourself by connecting with your breath and body.

3. On one of your papers, write a list of anything that happened throughout the year that was difficult or painful for you. Write as much as you need to get it all out. Allow any emotions that come up to flow through you without judgment. If you are using snowflake obsidian, keep it near you as you write this list.

4. When your list is made, fold it up, and hold it to your heart.

5. Repeat this phrase, or something like it, aloud or in your head, "I accept the challenges this year brought and trust I will heal and learn from them. I release these hardships into the fire to be transformed. So it is."

6. Light your paper and place it in your fireproof dish or into a bonfire or fireplace. *Note*: Always practice fire safety. Never leave a fire or your paper burning unattended. Ensure that you have proper ventilation if you are not burning your paper outside.

7. Allow yourself to release any more emotions around letting your hardships go. Let yourself release in any way that feels natural to you. This could be yelling, moving your body (dancing, yoga, etc.), or crying.

8. Notice whether you feel any lighter. If you don't, that's okay. Trust that you will soon.

9. When you feel ready, get your other paper, pen or pencil, and malachite if you're working with this stone.

10. Begin to write a list of what you're most grateful for. There's nothing too big or too small. Allow your gratitude to begin to transform any pain you experienced in the previous year into hope.

11. Write for as long as you want. When you're done, fold up your paper and place it under your malachite stone, or, if you're not using the malachite, simply place it on your altar.

CHAPTER 5

IMBOLC

WELCOME THE LIGHT AND
OPEN YOURSELF UP TO
NEW BEGINNINGS.

mbolc brings light and hope. The sun is shining a little brighter and warmer each day; it may still be cold outside, but the earth is beginning to show signs of awakening. This cross-quarter celebration marks the halfway point between the winter solstice and the spring equinox. In the northern hemisphere, Imbolc is celebrated on February 1 to 2 and August 1 to 2 in the southern hemisphere.

The word *imbolc* translates to "in the belly," which is significant for a couple of reasons. This season is often called "the quickening," referring to the time in utero when a mother first begins to feel her baby's movement. Nature is similar during this season because it shows the very first stirrings of life in this new cycle. "In the belly" also refers to pregnant ewes during this time. For our ancestors, the pregnant ewes were a welcome and life-giving sign. The ewe milk would be used for cheeses and butter to help nourish the community's frailest members.

Nature begins to show signs of waking during Imbolc. Even amidst a harsh winter, this season reminds us that life always finds a way. For our ancestors, these early signs of the coming of spring would bring hope and joy. The goddess Brigid is tightly woven into this celebration. Brigid is associated with fertility, health, protection, wisdom, inspiration, and fire. She was thought to come during Imbolc to offer healing and strength to those in need, even the animals.

CANDLEMAS AND ST. BRIGID

Imbolc is sometimes referred to as Candlemas. Some seasonal
celebrations, gods, and goddesses from pre-Christian times
were so popular and deeply embedded that they were
reworked into Christian celebrations. Many believe Candlemas
is one such celebration. Even the goddess Brigid is referenced
as St. Brigid in the story of Candlemas.

IMBOLC CORRESPONDENCES

·•◊ THEMES ◊•·
New beginnings, health, regeneration, hearth, ideas, inspiration

·•◊ MOON PHASE ◊•·
Waxing crescent

·•◊ CRYSTALS ◊•·
Green opal, kyanite, moss agate, green aventurine, quartz

·•◊ COLORS ◊•·
Green, white, yellow

·•◊ TOOLS & SPECIAL ITEMS ◊•·
Candles, fire, Brigid's cross, white fabric, besom (broom)

·•◊ PLANTS & SCENTS ◊•·
Rosemary, bay leaf, lavender, angelica, basil

·•◊ FOODS ◊•·
Milk, cheese, butter

·•◊ RUNES ◊•·
Wunjo, Uruz, Sowilo, Kenaz

·•◊ ZODIAC ◊•·
Aquarius

·•◊ GODS AND GODDESSES ◊•·
Eros, Aengus Og, Bragi, Brigid, Arianrhod, Athena, Danu, Selene, Hestia

CONNECTING WITH THE ENERGY OF IMBOLC

Energetically, Imbolc is a season to breathe in inspiration and begin taking action toward your desires. It's a time to cleanse, both physically and energetically, to remove anything that could be holding you back from taking clear action toward your desires. If you need to make changes to improve your mental or physical health, now is the time to make those changes and seek the support you need. This season is also a time to honor the hearth and home. Creating a sacred space in the home creates a stable space in which you can grow. You could even call on Brigid to come to your side.

The energy of Imbolc calls you to begin planning and getting crystal clear about what you want to birth into existence. It might be time to take action, or it might not. The important piece here is that you get clear about what you want so you can plan accordingly. As the earth begins to wake up, it's time for you to be open to seeing things in a new light too. Energetically, you could view this as a time to be aware of how you're spending your time, both mentally and physically. Have you been on autopilot? If you have, it may be time to do things that inspire you to continue to grow.

OPEN YOURSELF UP TO INSPIRATION AND
NEW PATHS UNSEEN.

There are several ways to work with the energy of this season, including cleaning your house both energetically and physically, writing lists of things that need to be done to progress your goals, tending to your physical health, and enjoying activities that inspire you. The goddess Brigid can be called upon during this season to bring you energy and inspiration. Fire will be a key theme in connecting with both the goddess Brigid and this season's energy. Use the following journal prompts, card spread, and meditation to help you get inspired and begin taking action toward your goals.

·•◊ TIP ◊•·

Call in inspiration to propel you through the final days of winter. Write a list of projects or hobbies that you feel inspired to begin and select to start working towards. Keep your list somewhere visible as a reminder to welcome inspiration.

IMBOLC AND THE WAXING CRESCENT MOON

Imbolc is associated with the waxing crescent moon phase. This phase comes right after the new moon and signals the very beginning phases of taking action. It's time to begin the early planning stages of any projects you'd like to focus on for the year ahead. Similar to the idea of focusing on the hearth and home during this season, the waxing crescent phase invites you to prepare and get ready to spring into action.

IMBOLC JOURNAL
REFLECTIONS

Use these journal prompts to explore your relationship
with hope and inspiration for the year ahead.

- What am I most hopeful about right now?

- What or who inspires me the most and why?

- Is there anything I need or want to do to improve my
  mental or physical health?

- What steps will I need to take to find more healing in
  these areas?

- What's one goal I'd
  like to accomplish in
  the next year? List five
  things I'll need to do to
  accomplish it.

IMBOLC CARD SPREAD

This three-card spread is intended to help you hone in on your desires, find inspiration to move forward, and assess possible blocks that may arise. Perform this card spread with your favorite oracle or tarot card deck.

1. Where should I be focusing my energy to move closer to my desires?

2. Where can I find more inspiration around my desires?

3. How can I best move through any blocks that arise?

IMBOLC SPROUTING SEED MEDITATION

For this meditation, you'll focus on being open to new possibilities. Set aside 10 to 20 minutes to perform this meditation. If you'd like to hold some crystals in your hands or place some nearby during this meditation, clear quartz, green aventurine, and moss agate are all great options.

1. Take a comfortable seat, close your eyes, and spend 1 to 2 minutes centering yourself by tuning in to your body and breath.

2. Begin to send your breath deep into your low belly with each inhale, then exhale slowly. Repeat this five times.

3. Release any control over your breath and let your breath do what it wants to for the remainder of the meditation.

4. Begin to visualize a tiny seed in the cold ground. Let the image of the seed begin to unfold and grow within your mind's eye.

5. Imagine the seedling breaking through the shell of its seed and beginning its journey toward the surface of the earth.

6. Then, imagine the tiny sprout breaking through the soil of the earth to start receiving sunlight.

7. Imagine yourself as this tiny energetic seed, growing into a new plant.

8. Just like the seedling of your imagination, visualize yourself soaking in the sunlight of a new day.

9. Bask in the light of new growth, hope, and possibility.

10. Stay in this light-filled space for as long as you like.

11. When you're ready, open your eyes, and tune back in to your physical body.

RITUALS FOR IMBOLC

To celebrate this season's energy, rituals revolve around the hearth, health, and inspiration. Here's a list of traditional rituals associated with the season of Imbolc and a more in-depth ritual to try.

- Connect with the goddess Brigid.

- Make Brigid's cross or sun wheel.

- Light a white candle in honor of the growing light of the sun.

- Give an offering to Brigid, such as a cup of milk.

- Energetically cleanse your home, altar, and any sacred tools.

- Hang a white cloth or scarf outside on the eve of Imbolc for Brigid to imbue with healing energy.

- Burn any evergreens in your home or on your altar from Yule.

CLEANSING CANDLE RITUAL FOR INSPIRATION

This is a great candle ritual to perform after you've energetically cleansed your space. For this Imbolc ritual, you'll call on the goddess Brigid to stir inspiration within you.

You'll need:

- A sharp tool to inscribe your candle with

- A white candle

- Anointing oil for your candle (whatever you have on hand works, such as almond oil or even olive oil; for an extra layer of energy, try rosemary oil, chamomile oil, or basil oil)

- Rosemary for cleansing (optional)

- Bay leaf for success (optional)

- Fireproof dish to burn your candle

- Matches or lighter

Steps:

1. Prepare all of your items and take a moment to center yourself by tuning in to your body and focusing on your breath.

2. Using your carving tool, write "inspire me" on your white candle. As you carve your candle, visualize yourself opening up to receiving insight and wisdom. *Note*: Please use caution when handling sharp tools.

3. Rub your anointing oil over your candle and continue to visualize yourself opening up to receive inspiration from spirit.

4. Roll your candle in any herbs you're using, or sprinkle them on top.

5. Place your candle in a fireproof dish or holder and light your candle.

6. When you light your candle, call on the goddess Brigid to join you, inspire you, and heal you. You might say something like, "Goddess Brigid, I welcome your light into this space. I am open to your inspiration and healing. So it is."

7. Stay with your candle as it burns. Take 2 to 5 minutes to sit with your candle and softly gaze at the flame. *Note*: Always use proper fire safety and care when working with candles. Never leave your candle unattended.

8. As the candle continues to burn, you can continue to meditate and connect with Brigid, write down any ideas that come to mind, or simply rest and enjoy the healing light of the goddess.

9. When the candle is done burning, take a moment to thank Brigid for joining you and thank yourself for taking the time to connect with the season.

CHAPTER 6

OSTARA

THE EARTH IS FERTILE
FOR NEW LIFE AND
NEW DREAMS.

The expansion of nature is in full swing. The earth is fertile and bursting with new life. Ostara is here to bring beauty, growth, fertile grounds, and a carefree sense of play. Ostara comes at the spring equinox, which marks a special time of equal day and night. The equinox makes this season inherently about balance as well. Ostara is celebrated between March 20 and 23, depending on the calendar year, in the northern hemisphere and between September 20 and 23 in the southern hemisphere.

Ostara marks the most fertile period on the Wheel of the Year. The goddess associated with this season is Ostara, also called Eostre, and symbolizes fertility herself. She is related to the moon, fertility, spring, and growth. Ostara corresponds to the maiden energy of the Triple Goddess (maiden, mother, crone). The archetype of the maiden calls you to allow for expansion and savor your beauty. Her name translates to "dawn," but unlike Yule, dawn in this situation is associated with the dawn of the fertile period and spring. For our ancestors, this time would be filled with joy, happiness, and busy preparations for the growing season.

For our ancestors, the dawn of spring is a reason to celebrate. Warmer days brought a greater likelihood of survival and the ability to thrive.

The energy of Ostara is one of celebration and reverence for both the light and the dark of life. As you take concerted steps toward your goals, Ostara offers you a moment of reflection to celebrate how far you've come and honor where you came from. This season also brings an energy of playfulness and joy.

OSTARA AND EASTER

The celebration of Ostara has been worked into several of our modern-day festivities. We see it most prominently in the celebration of Easter, the Easter bunny, and decorating eggs. Eggs and hares have long been a sacred part of this celebration and are closely associated with the goddess Ostara and fertility. Some believe the name of the holiday itself was modeled after the name Eostre, which is another name for the Goddess Ostara.

OSTARA
CORRESPONDENCES

·•◊ THEMES ◊•·
Fertility, growth, love, self-care, play, beauty, balance

·•◊ MOON PHASE ◊•·
First quarter moon

·•◊ ELEMENT ◊•·
Air

·•◊ CRYSTALS ◊•·
Rose quartz, rhodonite, unakite, pink or green tourmaline, sodalite

·•◊ COLORS ◊•·
Pink, yellow, green, pastel hues

·•◊ TOOLS & SPECIAL ITEMS ◊•·
Herbal smoke, fresh flowers, eggs, images of rabbits

·•◊ PLANTS & SCENTS ◊•·
Violet, rose, lily, jasmine, honeysuckle, daffodil

·•◊ FOODS ◊•·
Eggs

·•◊ RUNES ◊•·
Berkana, Dagaz, Inguz, Laguz, Wunjo, Gebo

·•◊ ZODIAC ◊•·
Pisces, Aries

·•◊ GODS AND GODDESSES ◊•·
Adonis, Attis, Daghda, Eostre or Ostara, Eos, Aphrodite, Artemis, Cybele

CONNECTING WITH THE ENERGY OF OSTARA

At the heart of Ostara is a calling for you to connect with the beauty around you and within you. Honoring this season's energy can be as simple as going for a walk, smelling fresh flowers, and enjoying nature. Ostara invites you to notice and enjoy your inner and outer beauty to bring the energy of this season to a more personal level. When was the last time you took stock of your gifts or gazed in awe at your incredible human body? When you honor yourself in these ways, you naturally feel more abundant.

FEEL THE ENERGY OF NEW LIFE BLOSSOMING ALL AROUND YOU!

The active energy of this Sabbat is an opportunity to focus more directly on your goals and desires. Spring brings a powerful momentum that you can grab on to and work alongside as both you and the moon grow and expand. If you've had an inner knowing or nudge to pursue something new, whether it be a job, relationship, or creative activity, this season is a call to begin and allow. This is a good time to ask yourself whether there's anything you've been putting off that you truly feel called to act on. If you have felt such a call, this season is an invitation to love yourself enough to act.

OSTARA AND THE
FIRST QUARTER MOON

When we compare the Wheel of the Year to the moon phases, Ostara is associated with the first quarter moon, which is connected to the maiden archetype of the Triple Goddess. Maiden's energy is open and curious. She seeks new experiences to allow her continuous unfolding. This moon phase is also associated with action and is a reminder to continue acting according to your desires.

OSTARA JOURNAL REFLECTIONS

Use these journal prompts to help you identify things and activities that bring you joy and a sense of playfulness.

- ◆ What do I most love about myself?

- ◆ In what areas of my life would I most like to expand?

- ◆ What goals and desires are underway right now? How do I feel about them?

- ◆ How can I instill more play and happiness in my daily life?

- ◆ How might more play affect my ability to be more balanced in my life?

OSTARA CARD SPREAD

This four-card spread is intended to help you identify your deepest desires. Perform this card spread with your favorite oracle or tarot card deck.

1. What areas of my life seek to expand?

2. How can I help foster growth in this area?

3. What areas of my life need more balance?

4. How can I better honor my beauty and gifts?

RITUALS FOR OSTARA

To celebrate the energy of this season, rituals revolve around fertility, growth, and beauty. Here's a list of traditional rituals associated with the season of Ostara and a more in-depth ritual to try.

- ♦ Decorate eggs.

- ♦ Connect with the goddess Eostre.

- ♦ Decorate your home with spring flowers.

- ♦ Enjoy the spring weather.

- ♦ Play and do things that bring you joy.

- ♦ Perform manifesting spells and magick.

- ♦ Decorate your home with images of hares.

OSTARA FERTILE GROUND MEDITATION

For this meditation, you'll focus on self-love and cultivating fertile grounds within your life. Set aside 10 to 20 minutes to perform this meditation. If you'd like to hold some crystals in your hands or place some nearby during this meditation, kunzite, rose quartz, or unakite are all great options.

1. Take a comfortable seat, close your eyes, and spend 1 to 2 minutes centering yourself by tuning in to your body and breath.

2. Extend the length of your inhales and exhales, so they're equal in length.

3. Focus on your heart space and visualize a brilliant green glowing light around your heart area.

4. Visualize this green light growing in intensity and size with each inhale and exhale until your entire body is consumed by the lush green color.

5. Repeat the phrase, or something like it, aloud or in your mind, "My life is growing and unfolding beautifully. I trust my process."

6. Visualize little sprouts from the earth growing all around you and blossoming into beautiful flowers until you're surrounded by lovely blooms.

7. Stay in this lush and fertile visualization for as long as you'd like and soak up the energy of love and growth.

8. When you feel ready to end the meditation, release any control over your breath and allow it to return to normal.

9. Thank the flowers' energy for sharing their life with you and send them back into the earth. You may choose to release or to keep the visualization of the green light around your body.

10. Slowly open your eyes and take 1 to 2 minutes to connect with your body again before returning to your day.

FLORAL SELF-LOVE POTION

Because this season welcomes fertility, it is a great time to invite in more self-care and self-love. When you tend to your inner garden, you create fertile grounds for growth. This self-love potion is intended to embody the energy of the season and inspire a sense of self-love. Use it as a perfume or as a massage oil for yourself or others.

You'll need:

- A small glass bottle 4 to 6 ounces in size

- Enough carrier oil to fill two-thirds of your bottle (options include sweet almond oil, fractionated coconut oil, or jojoba oil)

- 1 to 3 pieces of rose quartz small enough to fit in your bottle

- Dried spring flowers from your area or store-bought

- 10 drops of each floral essential oil of your choice (rose, lavender, violet, lilac, honeysuckle, jasmine, or any other scent you associate with spring works well)

Steps:

1. Collect your items and take a few moments to ground and center yourself by taking three deep breaths.

2. Hold the intention in your mind to honor and love yourself to lay fertile grounds for creation. If visualizations come naturally to you, you can visualize yourself glowing with pink, loving light as you create your self-love potion.

3. Fill your glass bottle two-thirds of the way with your carrier oil.

4. One at a time, add your rose quartz and flowers. As you add each item to your bottle of carrier oil, say something you love about yourself.

5. Add 10 drops of the essential oils you've selected for your potion.

6. Hold the bottle in your hands and repeat this phrase, or something like it: "I love and honor my body, my mind, and my spirit. So it is."

7. As you use your oil as a perfume or for self-massage, connect with your self-love intention to create fertile grounds. As always, test a small portion of your skin for a reaction before spreading the oil on your body.

CHAPTER 7

BELTANE

LET YOUR PASSIONS
LEAD THE WAY.

Beltane, or May Day, brings a powerful surge of energy, passion, and action. This fire festival is the midway point between the spring equinox and the summer solstice and marks the summer season. The light and warmth of the sun are steadily growing, and so can your internal fires and passions. This energetic Sabbat is honored from April 30 to May 1 in the northern hemisphere and October 31 to November 1 in the southern hemisphere.

Most practitioners believe that the name Beltane comes from the "fires of Bel." Bel, also called Belenus, is the sun god in Celtic lore. The connection of Bel to Beltane indicates the importance of fire and the sun during this season. Beltane also falls opposite Samhain on the Wheel. This is a strong time to connect with the spirit realm. Like Samhain, the veil between the physical and spiritual world is thinner than usual during this season. For these reasons, Beltane was and still is a powerful and popular celebration.

For our ancestors, Beltane ushered in the beginning of the summer season, especially regarding the care of livestock. Therefore, many Beltane celebrations often included bonfire ceremonies where livestock would be ushered in between two fires to ensure a successful season. Love, passion, and unions were also a prominent part of this celebration. It was common for there to be a surge in marriage announcements, pregnancies, and passion-filled unions during Beltane.

BELTANE CORRESPONDENCES

·•◊ THEMES ◊•·
Passion, action, creativity, lust, sexuality, marriage, pleasure

·•◊ MOON PHASE ◊•·
Waxing gibbous

·•◊ CRYSTALS ◊•·
Carnelian, garnet, ruby, orange calcite, protective crystals
like onyx or black tourmaline

·•◊ COLORS ◊•·
Red, orange, yellow, green

·•◊ TOOLS & SPECIAL ITEMS ◊•·
Bonfire, candles, maypole, symbols representing fertility, spring flowers

·•◊ PLANTS & SCENTS ◊•·
Hawthorn, rose, honeysuckle, lilac, angelica

·•◊ FOODS ◊•·
Fresh herbs

·•◊ RUNES ◊•·
Berkana, Ehwaz, Algiz, Raidho, Uruz

·•◊ ZODIAC ◊•·
Taurus

·•◊ GODS AND GODDESSES ◊•·
Bel or Belenus, Balder, Cernunnos, Eros, Odin, Freya, Aphrodite, Artemis,
Blodeuwedd, Rhiannon, Frigga, Flora

CONNECTING WITH THE ENERGY OF BELTANE

The energy of this season is one of passion, action, and spiritual connection. Because Beltane comes right before Litha, the longest day of the year, this season is a powerful crescendo of energy leading up to the summer solstice. This season calls you to ignite your internal fires and find passion and pleasure all around you. Though the passion of Beltane is often associated with romantic lust, this energy can certainly be applied to your life with or without a romantic partner. Alternatively, if you have been working toward a goal, this season offers an energetic push to help you complete it.

Working with fire is a potent way to invoke the energy of Beltane. Fire represents the powerful masculine energy associated with this season. This could be done by having a bonfire celebration with friends or on a smaller scale with candles if honoring this Sabbat solo. Working with the energy of fire can be done metaphorically as well. The fire element is associated with the solar plexus area (above the belly button and below the heart center). Focusing on the solar plexus by building internal heat from exercises, breathwork practices, or solar plexus visualizations can help connect with this Sabbat's energy.

STIR YOUR INTERNAL FIRE TO
SPARK YOUR TRANSFORMATION.

BELTANE AND THE WAXING GIBBOUS MOON

The waxing gibbous is the moon phase that occurs right before the full moon. The energy of this lunar phase is an intense stage of growth. It offers a final push of energy to accomplish goals and refine final projects. Regarding the Triple Goddess (maiden, mother, crone) aspect, this phase comes right before the mother archetype. It is therefore associated with the energy of the maiden on the precipice of motherhood. The waxing gibbous moon and Beltane represent the very process of transforming.

Another important facet of this season is pleasure, which
corresponds to water and the sacral region. This watery and
creative energy is the feminine energy associated with Beltane. We
can see both of these energies represented in the maypole, the
phallic stick that corresponds to masculine energy and the circle
at the top that corresponds to feminine energy. To connect to the
pleasurable energy associated with this season, you'll find water
and the sacral center to be helpful. Water's flowing energy is the
creative force of the womb space and is associated with pleasure,
fertility, and creation. You can connect with this energy through
the physical element of water or embody the water element
through dance, sexuality, and pleasurable activities. Use the
following journal prompts, card spread, and meditation to explore
and deepen your passions.

BELTANE JOURNAL REFLECTIONS

Use these journal prompts to explore your relationship with passion and divine feminine and masculine energies.

- ◆ Where do I find the most pleasure and joy in my life right now?

- ◆ How can I bring more pleasure and joy into my life?

- ◆ How do I feel about current projects in my life? If they've lost their appeal, how can I reinvigorate them?

- ◆ How can I honor the divine masculine energy more in my life?

- ◆ How can I honor the divine feminine energy more in my life?

BELTANE CARD SPREAD

This five-card spread is intended to help you cultivate more pleasure in your life. Perform this card spread with your favorite oracle or tarot card deck.

1. In what areas of my life am I cutting myself off from pleasure?

2. How can I find more pleasure in my life?

3. What area of my life would benefit from more masculine or fire energy?

4. What area of my life would benefit from more feminine or water energy?

5. What areas of my life will expand when I allow more pleasure, creation, and energy to flow through me?

RITUALS FOR BELTANE

To celebrate this season's energy, rituals revolve around pleasure, joy, sensuality, and the fertile earth. Here's a list of common rituals associated with the season of Beltane and a more in-depth ritual to try.

- Make a flower crown.

- Decorate your home with flowers.

- Play in nature.

- Dance around a maypole or make a maypole for your altar.

- Leave an offering for the Faeries.

- Explore your sensuality.

- Have or attend a bonfire.

- Wash your face with morning dew from plants and flowers.

- Practice both love and protection spells.

BELTANE PASSION MEDITATION

For this meditation, you'll focus on sparking a fire of passion within yourself. This could be a passion for yourself, someone else, or a project. Set aside 10 to 20 minutes to perform this meditation. If you'd like to hold some crystals in your hands during this meditation, carnelian, orange calcite, and garnet are all great options. I suggest deciding what area of your life you'd like to bring more passion to before starting.

1. Take a comfortable seat, close your eyes, and tune in to your breath and physical body.

2. Begin to lengthen your inhales and exhales.

3. Make your inhales and exhales equal in length for a count of four seconds each. These are shorter breaths intended to warm your body. Make sure you are breathing from your low belly. If you become lightheaded, stop and take a break. Do this for 3 to 5 minutes.

4. Once 3 to 5 minutes have passed, release any control over the breath and breathe normally.

5. Bring your focus to your solar plexus area, which is above your belly button and below your heart space.

6. Visualize an orange and yellow flame in your solar plexus area.

7. Bring to mind something or someone you'd like to bring more passion to. Hold the vision in your mind.

8. With each breath, visualize the light of the orange flame growing in size until it fully consumes your body.

9. Imagine the warmth of the flame warming your body and lighting a fire of passion within you.

10. Stay in the meditation for as long as you like.

11. When you're ready, open your eyes. Know that this energy and passion are always available to you.

BELTANE BEAUTY
FACE MIST

This beauty recipe is based on the old ritual of young women washing their faces with the hawthorn tree's dew on Beltane. If you have a hawthorn tree nearby, that's great, but any morning dew from the grass or a plant will work for this recipe. This is a great spray to make and use on and around Beltane to connect with this season's energy.

You'll need:

- ◆ 1 to 1½ ounces of rose water (use 1 ounce if you intend to add fresh rose petals to your mist)

- ◆ ½ ounce of alcohol-free witch hazel

- ◆ 2 to 3 drops of vitamin E oil (optional)

- ◆ A 2-ounce spray bottle

- ◆ 1 to 3 drops of dew from any plants or grass on or around Beltane

- ◆ Fresh rose petals (optional)

Steps:

1. Add your rose water, witch hazel, and vitamin E oil (if using) to your bottle.

2. Collect your fresh dew and add a few drops to your bottle. This step is more about infusing your mist with the energy of this season, so a tiny amount will do.

3. Add your rose petals if you're using them.

4. Hold your bottle in your hands to infuse it with an energy of beauty and pleasure.

5. Test your face mist on a small portion of your skin before using it on your entire face to ensure your skin doesn't have a reaction.

6. Mist your face in the morning with or without makeup. Give your face a spritz anytime you'd like a little refresh.

CHAPTER 8

LITHA

BASK IN THE WARMTH
AND POWER OF THE SUN.

itha, also called midsummer, honors the height of the summer season and our life-giving sun. Litha is one of four solar festivals, which also marks the summer solstice and the longest day of the year. This celebratory Sabbat calls us to find gratitude for everything that is possible through the light and warmth of the sun. Litha is honored on the summer solstice, which usually falls between June 20 and 24 in the northern hemisphere and between December 20 and 24 in the southern hemisphere.

Like the winter solstice, it's easy to find evidence indicating how important the summer solstice was for our ancestors. There are ancient sites around the world that line up with the rising solstice sun. The word *solstice* actually means "sun stands still." During the solstices, the sun appears to stand still in the sky, which our ancestors, no doubt, noticed. It is also at this point that the days start to decrease in light. Similar to Yule, Litha offers an opportunity to appreciate the duality of both light and shadow present within us and our world.

Strength and power are both themes of Litha. The height of daylight propels nature into a flurry of growth and activity. For our ancestors, this palpable season of production was a reason to celebrate and hope for a full harvest in the coming months. The cold of the winter is out of sight, and the growing season's hard work is starting to bear fruit. To properly honor the sun, it's a common practice to watch the sun rise and set on the day of the summer solstice and hold a large bonfire during the night of the summer solstice.

···❨ ❩···

STAND IN YOUR POWER. RADIATE YOUR TRUE SELF.

···❨ ❩···

Beyond honoring the potent energy of the sun, Litha calls you to find ways to honor your vibrancy. How can you harness the energy within you to better shine your truest and boldest version of yourself out into the world? The invigorating energy of the sun can be harnessed and applied to any area of your life that needs a boost of confidence. It's a time to be bold in your actions and clear in your communication. Litha is also an opportunity to celebrate yourself, your gifts, and all of the growth you've done so far this year.

·❂ TIP ❂·

If it's cloudy or rainy where you live, light some candles inside as a show of gratitude for our life-giving sun.

LITHA CORRESPONDENCES

·•◊ THEMES ◊•·
Power, light, gratitude, confidence, strength

·•◊ MOON PHASE ◊•·
Full moon

·•◊ ELEMENT ◊•·
Fire

·•◊ CRYSTALS ◊•·
Citrine, sunstone, yellow jasper, rutilated quartz, hematite, sodalite, turquoise

·•◊ COLORS ◊•·
Gold, yellow, red, green, blue

·•◊ TOOLS & SPECIAL ITEMS ◊•·
Bonfire, candles, sun wheel

·•◊ PLANTS & SCENTS ◊•·
Oak tree, St. John's wort, elderflower, sunflower, chamomile, lavender, vervain

·•◊ FOODS ◊•·
Honey cake, fresh herbs from the season, edible flowers, mead

·•◊ RUNES ◊•·
Jera, Ehwaz, Sowilo, Wunjo

·•◊ ZODIAC ◊•·
Gemini, Cancer

·•◊ GODS AND GODDESSES ◊•·
Apollo, Lugh, the Oak King, Sulis, Sunna, Gréine

LITHA ALTAR

CONNECTING WITH THE ENERGY OF LITHA

The sun permeates every aspect of our lives. For this reason, you'll find that there's no shortage of ways to connect with the energy of Litha. Whether you go for a solo walk outside or plan an elaborate trip to the ocean, this Sabbat is definitely one to enjoy the radiant sun and the outdoors. Consider making a list of your favorite outdoor activities and decide which ones you'd like to do on your own or with a group for the summer solstice. Just make a point to spend time outside when the weather does clear up. You can also find lots of ways to honor the sun within the comfort of your home, which you'll find later in this chapter.

LET THE LIGHT OF THE SUN WARM YOUR SKIN AND SPARK A FIRE IN YOUR SPIRIT!

This season invites you to honor and celebrate your personal light, radiance, and beauty. It's a time to be bold in calling in what you desire and taking action toward your goals. Are there parts of yourself that you've been holding back or afraid to show off? Litha asks you to be confident in sharing who you are with the world. This is a great time to write a list of things that you're most proud of about yourself. Use the following journal prompts, card spread, and meditation to explore all of the hard work you've done and are currently still doing to be the truest version of yourself.

LITHA AND THE FULL MOON

On the Wheel of the Year, Litha corresponds to the full moon. Just like the moon in its fullest phase, the sun is at its height of power and strength for the season. When working with the moon phases, the full moon offers a time of heightened psychic energy. Litha can also be used as a time to practice intuitive and psychic work. If the full moon happens on or near Litha, you have some seriously magickal energy to work with! The full moon also represents the Triple Goddess mother archetype, which in Litha can be seen as nature coming into full maturity.

LITHA JOURNAL REFLECTIONS

Use these journal prompts to help you step into your power and honor your gifts for the summer solstice.

- ◆ What does summer invoke for me? How does it make me feel?

- ◆ What projects or ideas have I birthed into reality recently?

- ◆ How can I celebrate and honor the completion of any goals and desires I've been working toward?

- ◆ What are my favorite physical attributes and personality traits about myself?

- ◆ What activities give me a sense of power and strength?

LITHA CARD SPREAD

This six-card spread is intended to help you identify your strengths and how to better live your truth. Perform this card spread with your favorite oracle or tarot card deck.

1. What are my greatest strengths?

2. What is blocking me from fully embodying my strength?

3. How can I more fully step into my power?

4. Where do I need to set boundaries to better support my truth?

5. How will embodying my true gifts and power transform my life?

6. How will embodying my true gifts and power transform the world around me?

RITUALS FOR LITHA

To celebrate this season's energy, rituals revolve around confidence, strength, and honoring the sun. Here's a list of common rituals associated with the season of Litha and the summer solstice and a more in-depth ritual to try.

- ◆ Spend time outside.

- ◆ Make a honey cake or solar water.

- ◆ Make a sun wheel or decorate your home with symbols of the sun or bright flowers.

- ◆ Have or attend a bonfire.

- ◆ Drink or make mead.

- ◆ Light a candle to honor the light of the sun.

- ◆ Enjoy food using fresh herbs from the season.

LITHA LIGHT MEDITATION

For this meditation, you'll focus on celebrating your inner
light and connecting with the energy and light of the sun.
Set aside 10 to 20 minutes to perform this meditation. If
you'd like to hold some crystals in your hands during this
meditation, citrine and sunstone are great options.

1. Take a comfortable seat, close your eyes, and tune
   in to your breath and physical body.

2. Straighten your spine and roll your shoulders up
   and back.

3. Begin to lengthen your inhales and exhales.

4. Send your breath deep into your belly. Continue to
   breathe deeply throughout this meditation.

5. Visualize a stream of light coming from the sun and
   connecting to the crown of your head.

6. Feel this energy light up your entire body with warm,
   glowing white light from the inside out.

7. Bask in the power and energy of this light and feel it increase with each inhale and exhale that you take.

8. Bring to mind three things about yourself that you love or that bring you a sense of confidence.

9. Stay in this place of light, power, and confidence for as long as you'd like.

10. When you feel ready to come out of the meditation, feel the sun's energy slowly start to retreat while leaving your body glowing with radiance and power.

11. Release any control over your breath and slowly open your eyes. Tune in to the sense of power and confidence that you inspired within yourself anytime you need.

LITHA SOLAR WATER RITUAL

My favorite way to celebrate and partake in the sun's energy this time of year is to make solar water. Some practitioners believe that infusing your water with sunlight can give you a subtle energy boost and that is has an ionizing and antimicrobial effect on the water.

Though there's no hard proof of these benefits, it's certainly worth trying and won't do you any harm. Plus, it's super simple!

You'll need:

- ◆ A glass cup or pitcher

- ◆ Water (fresh spring water is best!)

- ◆ Fresh fruit and herbs of choice (optional)

Steps:

1. Fill your cup or pitcher with water.

2. Add any fresh fruit and herbs you'd like. My favorite combination is lemon slices, raspberries, and mint leaves.

3. Place your water out in the light of the midday sun, when the sun is at its height of power.

4. Leave your water in the sunlight for 15 to 60 minutes. If you live in a hot climate as I do, you'll only need to leave your water in the sun for 15 minutes. Otherwise, it might be too hot to drink!

5. Drink your solar water and feel your body become imbued with energy from the sun.

CHAPTER 9

LUGHNASADH

HARVEST THE FRUITS OF
YOUR LABOR AND BASK
IN YOUR GROWTH.

Lughnasadh (pronounced loo-na-sa), also known as Lammas, marks the first harvest of the year and is the halfway point between the summer solstice and the autumn equinox. The earth is still warm during this season, and though the daylight still outshines the night, it is shortening each day. This would mark the beginning of the harvest season for our ancestors, the first of three harvests for the year. Lughnasadh is celebrated on August 1 to 2 in the northern hemisphere and February 1 to 2 in the southern hemisphere.

The name Lughnasadh stems from the warrior god Lugh. Lugh is associated with the sun, craftsmanship, and warrior energy. For the cultures that celebrated this Sabbat as Lughnasadh, it would be in Lugh's honor. Lammas, a Christianized name for this Sabbat, is the other name commonly associated with this celebration. Lammas is also referred to as Loaf Mass Day. It was, and still is, common practice in parts of northern Europe to bake a special loaf of bread from the first grain harvest. Though Lughnasadh is where this Sabbat began, each name associated with the first harvest tells a story about this season. Lugh offers the pride and energy associated with harvesting grain crops, while Lammas focuses on the importance of grains as a life-giving food source.

At this point in the cycle of the year, the cocreation of food from farming and nature's magick has been happening for many months. The harvest seasons were vital for our ancestors because the grains from them would support communities and livestock for the cold winter months ahead. First harvests meant hard work, celebration, and a reverence for the earth, and Lughnasadh calls us to have deep gratitude for Mother Nature.

The energy of this season is one of pride, success, and gratitude. The harvesting of crops during this season is a huge accomplishment that our ancestors would have been extremely proud of. The god Lugh reflects the sentiment of pride because of his association with craftsmanship. This season invites you to not only notice where your efforts are bearing fruit but also to be proud of the results.

If you're not the type to revel in your successes, no matter how small they are, this season calls you to embody the energy of pride. If you never take time to appreciate your hard work, you may end up passing right over the very results you've been working toward. You deserve to be celebrated and to celebrate your successes, and this is the season to do so.

·•◠ TIP ◠•·

Write a list of your favorite qualities and skills you possess. Consider leaving your list somewhere you'll see it often, perhaps even on your altar.

LUGHNASADH CORRESPONDENCES

·•◠ THEMES ◠•·
Harvest, gratitude, pride, accomplishments, success, warriorhood

·•◠ MOON PHASE ◠•·
Waning gibbous

·•◠ CRYSTALS ◠•·
Tiger's eye, red jasper, pyrite, smoky quartz

·•◠ COLORS ◠•·
Gold, red, orange, purple, tan

·•◠ TOOLS & SPECIAL ITEMS ◠•·
Corn dolly, ritual bread, candles, fire, items that represent gratitude

·•◠ PLANTS & SCENTS ◠•·
Sunflower, calendula, vervain, hops, marigold, rosehips

·•◠ FOODS ◠•·
Wheat, corn, bread, beer, berries, seasonal fruits and vegetables

·•◠ RUNES ◠•·
Ansuz, Eihwaz, Fehu, Tiwaz

·•◠ ZODIAC ◠•·
Leo

·•◠ GODS AND GODDESSES ◠•·
Lugh, Aine, Ceres, Danu, Gaia

LUGHNASADH ALTAR

CONNECTING WITH THE ENERGY OF LUGHNASADH

Similar to Litha, this Sabbat can be spent outside connecting with the earth. Though the sun is still high and hot, this season invites you to enjoy and give gratitude to the abundance of Mother Earth. If you farm or garden, the harvesting energy may be quite literal for you this time of year. If farming or gardening isn't a part of your life, go for a walk and notice what plants are blooming or fruiting. On a more personal level, this is a good time to be aware of any areas of your life that may be ready to harvest. Are there projects or relationships that are showing results?

PAUSE AND DELIGHT IN HOW
FAR YOU HAVE COME.

To access the energy of pride associated with this season, celebrate something you've created or accomplished. Alternatively, this is also a great time to pick up a hobby, sport, or passion that's new to you. If there's something you've been putting off that you've felt called to do, accomplishing it will undoubtedly fill you with a sense of pride. The very act of trying something new, regardless of the end results, is something to be proud of. This season is not a time to be shy about your accomplishments.

LUGHNASADH AND THE
WANING GIBBOUS MOON

The season of Lughnasadh is associated with the waning gibbous moon. This phase comes right after the full moon and begins the moon's waning. Just like the sun at this time of year, the moon in her waning phase will begin to shrink in light. This is a time to pause and notice all that has happened up until this phase. It is also a time to seek gratitude, even if your plans may not have gone exactly as you hoped.

LUGHNASADH JOURNAL REFLECTIONS

Use these journal prompts to better understand your relationship with pride during Lughnasadh.

- ♦ What is my relationship with pride like? Do I feel safe to be proud of myself, or do I hide my pride?

- ♦ What am I most proud of myself for right now?

- ♦ What's a new hobby or skill I'd like to learn that would give me a sense of pride?

- ♦ Where do I see the fruits of my hard work? Are there areas of my life ready to be harvested?

- ♦ What harvests in my life am I most grateful for?

LUGHNASADH CARD SPREAD

This five-card spread is intended to help you identify parts of your life that are maturing and ready to be harvested and help you continue moving toward mastery. Perform this card spread with your favorite oracle or tarot card deck.

1. What areas of my life are ready to mature?

2. How will advancing into maturity in this area change my life?

3. In what areas am I holding myself back from advancing?

4. In what area of my life should I work toward mastery?

5. How will having a healthy sense of pride help me step into a more mature role?

RITUALS FOR LUGHNASADH

To help you celebrate the energy of this season, rituals revolve around pride, success, and harvesting. Here's a list of common rituals associated with the season of Lughnasadh and one in-depth ritual to try.

- ♦ Spend time outside.

- ♦ Bake bread.

- ♦ Decorate your home with grains.

- ♦ Make a corn dolly.

- ♦ Connect with the god Lugh.

- ♦ Learn a new skill.

- ♦ Perform spells and magick for abundance.

LUGHNASADH HARVEST MEDITATION

For this meditation, you'll call in the harvests from all of your efforts this year. Set aside 10 to 20 minutes to perform this meditation. If you'd like to hold some crystals in your hands during this meditation, tiger's eye and pyrite are great options.

1. Take a comfortable seat, close your eyes, and tune in to your breath and physical body.

2. Focus on your breath and take three big belly breaths.

3. Bring something to mind that you've been working toward. Think about what you are hoping to accomplish with this goal.

4. Visualize a gold sphere spinning in your heart space, radiating golden light in all directions.

5. Imagine that this gold spinning sphere is magnetic and pulling in your desires.

6. Visualize what you would feel like to accomplish the goal that you called to mind. How would you feel when it's done? If it's a goal tied to physical things, what would you have in your life when you accomplish this goal?

7. Feel the golden energy pulling everything toward you with ease.

8. Hold the visualization of the golden light and all of your desires coming to fruition.

9. Stay in this space and breathe for as long as you'd like.

10. When you're ready to end the meditation, feel the magnetism of the golden light stay with you, continuing to pull in your desires.

11. Open your eyes and connect with your body.

ABUNDANCE CHARM BAG

Lughnasadh is the first of three harvest seasons, so this is a great time to perform spells and rituals for abundance. Charm bags are spells within a bag and will make your magick simple and portable. Keep in mind that abundance doesn't always refer to money, so you can perform this ritual to bring more abundance into any area of your life. This ritual is best performed during the waxing moon phase.

You'll need:

♦ Marker or paint to draw a symbol on the outside of your bag

♦ A green or gold cloth bag

♦ Piece of tiger's eye and/or pyrite

♦ A bay leaf, dried or fresh

♦ Basil, dried or fresh

♦ An acorn (optional)

♦ Money or something else that symbolizes what you're calling in

Steps:

1. Collect and prepare all of your items.

2. Call to mind what you'd like to bring into your life for this spell.

3. Draw or paint the Fehu rune (a symbol of abundance, seen on the on the bag in the image below) or any other symbol representing abundance to you on the outside of your bag.

4. Begin to place your items in your bag. As you place each item in your spell bag, visualize what you'll feel like when you receive what you're calling in.

5. When all of the items are in your bag, hold the bag in your hands and say the following, or something similar, aloud or in your mind, "Everything in my highest and best good is on its way to me. So it is."

6. Place your bag on your altar or somewhere you'll see it regularly.

CHAPTER 10

MABON

FIND GRATITUDE IN
THE BALANCE OF
LIGHT AND DARKNESS.

The harvest season is in full force at the time of Mabon, the second of three harvest celebrations. Mabon falls on the autumn equinox, when daylight and night strike a balance and are equal in length. Moving forward from the autumn equinox, the nights progressively get darker as we approach winter. Mabon is celebrated between September 20 and 23, depending on the calendar year, in the northern hemisphere and between March 20 and 23 in the southern hemisphere.

Mabon is a modern name that was given to this celebration in the 1970s by Aiden Kelly. The name Mabon comes from a Welsh mythological figure named Mabon ap Modron. Mabon did not have any clear connection to the autumn equinox, so we may never know why this name stuck, other than the fact that Aidan and others wanted a short name for this Sabbat to better match the other quarter celebrations. Some who work with the Wheel of the Year choose to simply call this celebration the autumn or autumnal equinox.

The autumn equinox brings a strong sense of balance. Mabon falls in the middle of the harvest season, and there's a sense of finding balance between celebrating the harvest and the very real need to prepare for the coming winter. The full moon closest to the equinox is often referred to as the harvest moon. For some of our ancestors, the harvest moon meant working in the crops from sun up through the night by the light of the moon. This harvest season was full of deep gratitude and hard work to ensure the prosperity of life.

There is also a theme of wholeness that runs through Mabon. This sense of completion comes from the quickly approaching end of the growing season or the end of a cycle. When we seek to find a balance between light and dark, day and night, joy and sorrow, we can become more whole. Apples are tied to this season because they were viewed as a symbol of wholeness and were commonly harvested at the time of Mabon. When you cut an apple horizontally, the seeds create a five-pointed star, representing all five elements (air, earth, water, fire, and spirit). Even though apples are more closely related to sin in Christianity, they were, and still are, sacred symbols for many Celtic people.

·•◌ TIP ◌•·

As the seasonal year shifts into the darker and colder half of the year, spend some time taking stock of everything that's happened in your year so far. What are you most grateful for? What have been the most difficult parts of your year? Practice holding space for both the joy and the sorrow of your year. The autumn equinox is a reminder to allow more balance in your life. It's safe to celebrate, and it is also safe to mourn.

EVERY ENDING OFFERS A NEW PATH.

MABON CORRESPONDENCES

·•◊ THEMES ◊•·
Gratitude, harvest, abundance, balance, fulfillment, endings, preparation

·•◊ MOON PHASE ◊•·
Last quarter moon

·•◊ ELEMENT ◊•·
Water

·•◊ CRYSTALS ◊•·
Carnelian, snowflake obsidian, rhodonite, malachite, moonstone, yellow topaz

·•◊ COLORS ◊•·
Maroon, orange, brown, tan

·•◊ TOOLS & SPECIAL ITEMS ◊•·
Fall leaves, corn dolly, gourds

·•◊ PLANTS & SCENTS ◊•·
Yarrow, sage, cinnamon, patchouli, frankincense, anise

·•◊ FOODS ◊•·
Apples, grains, gourds, pumpkins, nuts, seeds, berries

·•◊ RUNES ◊•·
Gebo, Fehu, Mannaz, Sowilo

·•◊ ZODIAC ◊•·
Virgo, Libra

·•◊ GODS AND GODDESSES ◊•·
Avalloc, Dionysus, Mabon, Cailleach, Persephone, Inanna, Morrigan, Modron

CONNECTING WITH THE ENERGY OF MABON

The abundance associated with Mabon is an invitation to actively seek out gratitude. If you're like most modern humans, you're probably somewhat removed from your food and rely on grocery stores. There's nothing wrong with this, but learning about the places and people associated with your food production can be a powerful practice, especially during Mabon. Understanding where your food comes from will help you feel more connected and grateful for the food that keeps you alive. On a larger scale, this season calls us to become more aware of those around us who may be in need. If you don't already volunteer, this is a great time to make a plan to regularly offer mutual aid and community care. On a personal level, simple acts like creating a gratitude list or performing random acts of kindness can also help you open your heart to this season.

FIND GRATITUDE FOR EVERYTHING THAT HAS COME AND IS STILL COMING.

To tap into the energy of balance that this season offers, you may find it helpful to journal or make lists of areas of your life that feel out of balance. What areas of your life do you need to adjust to feel more balanced and at ease? If you feel out of touch with nature, it's time to build in time to be outside. If you've felt overwhelmed, what can you take off your plate or delegate to someone else? If you've been putting off doing something that needs to be done, it's time to commit yourself to finish. Use the following journal prompts, card spread, and meditation to be open and honest with yourself about why you are out of balance and what you need to do to find a better equilibrium.

MABON AND THE LAST QUARTER MOON

Mabon aligns with the last quarter moon phase, which brings an energy of shedding and letting go. In this phase, the moon is half light and half dark, again highlighting the sense of equal light and dark of this season. The last quarter moon calls you to release ways of being that are no longer serving you while also holding space for acceptance around anything that you're not able or ready to release.

MABON JOURNAL REFLECTIONS

Use these journal prompts to explore gratitude, balance, and wholeness for Mabon.

- ♦ What areas of my life are most abundant right now?

- ♦ What am I most grateful for in my life right now?

- ♦ What does wholeness mean to me on a personal level?

- ♦ Do I feel whole now or out of balance?

- ♦ What would I need to change in my life to find more balance and feel more whole?

MABON CARD SPREAD

This four-card spread is intended to help you identify parts of your life that are out of balance and help you find more gratitude and wholeness. Perform this card spread with your favorite oracle or tarot card deck.

1. How can I tap into more abundance in my life?

2. How will sharing my abundance with others help me grow?

3. What areas of my life are out of balance?

4. How can I find more wholeness in my life?

RITUALS FOR MABON

To celebrate the energy of this season, rituals revolve around gratitude and wholeness. Here's a list of traditional rituals associated with the season of Mabon and a more in-depth ritual to try.

♦ Make a corn dolly.

♦ Go apple picking.

♦ Decorate with fall items from nature.

♦ Perform rituals that center on gratitude, balance, and wholeness.

♦ Donate your time or money to someone in need.

♦ Bake bread or other items from grain.

♦ Give an offering to the earth.

MABON GRATITUDE MEDITATION

For this meditation, you'll cultivate gratitude. Set aside 10 to 20 minutes to perform this meditation. If you'd like to hold some crystals in your hands during this meditation, rhodonite and malachite are great options.

1. Take a comfortable seat, close your eyes, and tune in to your breath and physical body.

2. Focus on your breath and take three big belly breaths, releasing your exhales with an audible "ahhhhhh" sound.

3. Let your breath return to normal.

4. Focus on your heart space and visualize a green light growing around your heart.

5. Bring to mind something or someone you feel grateful for.

6. Place what you brought to mind into your heart space, as you feel your heart space expand with love and the green light.

7. Continue calling to mind people and things that bring you gratitude and placing them into your heart space. Do this until your visualization of the green light has filled up the entire room.

8. Bring three people to mind to send some of this loving green energy to.

9. Hold each person in your mind's eye and visualize them receiving the loving energy.

10. Stay in this space of love and gratitude for as long as you'd like.

11. When you're done, release the visualization and slowly open your eyes. Take a few moments to connect with your physical body before returning to your day.

CANDLE RITUAL FOR WHOLENESS AND BALANCE

Because Mabon falls on the autumn equinox, it offers an invitation to seek balance and a sense of wholeness. As discussed earlier, apples were commonly viewed as a symbol of wholeness.

You'll need:

- Pen or pencil

- A piece of paper

- Knife

- An apple

- Fireproof dish or vessel to safely burn your candle

- A brown candle (preferably a chime spell candle because it has a short burn time and will enable you to stay with your candle as it burns)

- Carving tool to carve into the candle wax

- Matches or lighter

- A journal

Steps:

1. Gather your materials and ensure that you won't be disturbed for 20 to 30 minutes.

2. Take 2 to 3 minutes to center and ground yourself. You can do this by tuning in to your body or focusing on your breathing for a couple of minutes.

3. Once you feel ready, bring to mind an area of your life that feels out of balance. Write this situation down on a piece of paper.

4. With a knife, cut your apple across the middle, and then cut a slice from that. Your slice should have a five-pointed star on it representing the five elements.

5. Place your paper in a fireproof dish. Place your apple slice on top.

6. Carve the word "whole" or the phrase "I am whole" into your candle with the knife or carving too.

7. Hold the brown candle in your hand and ask the earth to help bring you balance and wholeness.

8. Place your candle on top of the apple slice. You may need to carve a circle in your apple to ensure it stays upright.

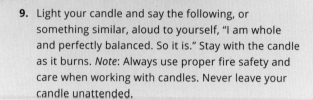

9. Light your candle and say the following, or something similar, aloud to yourself, "I am whole and perfectly balanced. So it is." Stay with the candle as it burns. *Note*: Always use proper fire safety and care when working with candles. Never leave your candle unattended.

10. As your candle burns, gaze at the flame and tune in to your breath and body.

11. Call in each of the five elements one at a time (earth, air, fire, water, and spirit) to restore you to wholeness and bring balance. Feel the support of the five elements around you.

12. Be open to any ideas that come to you to find more balance and wholeness in your life and write about them in your journal.

13. When your candle is done burning (if you're unable to stay with your candle until it's done, snuff it out with a candle snuffer to resume later), thank the elements one at a time for sharing their energy with you.

MESSAGE FROM THE AUTHOR

You are nature. As a species, we're increasingly separated from our food production, the seasons, and the natural world. This separation makes it easy to forget that we are nature. However, our magickal and cyclical world will continue its cycles with or without us. We are not integral to Mother Nature, but she is imperative to our well-being.

I hope that the suggestions within these pages spark a desire deep within to connect with the natural world more regularly. Within this regular appreciation and reverence for the natural world, we as a species will find ways to better care for ourselves and Mother Earth. Because, just like the seasons, healing is also cyclical.

Love ♥ Light

Cassie

THANK YOU

Endless gratitude to those who made this book series possible! Thank you to all of the sweet souls at Quarto Publishing, especially my editor, Keyla. Thank you to my designer, Sydney, who's been a creative force for Zenned Out since its inception many years ago. Sincere gratitude to my infinitely patient husband, who, unwaveringly and lovingly, supports every new journey I embark upon. Thank you to my mentor on my path of Celtic shamanism, Robin Afinowich. Eternal gratitude to my guides on the other side, including my sweet grandmother and father.

Thank you to every single one of my fans, followers, and supporters. I see you, and I love you. You light me up every day and give me the energy to continue sharing my gifts.

Love 🖤 Light

Cassie

ABOUT THE AUTHOR

Cassie Uhl is an artist, author, gentle guide to spirit, and lead goddess of her business, Zenned Out. She created Zenned Out with the mission to build a brand that normalizes spirituality. Her goal is to offer accessible information to enable you to understand a variety of spiritual practices and put them into action!

Inspired by her open-minded grandmother, Cassie has been meditating and working with her energy since her teenage years. Though she's always been inspired by nature, she began working more intuitively and magickally with nature in 2016 after losing her native British-born grandmother. Losing her grandmother spurred Cassie to reclaim her spiritual heritage, engross herself in the seasonal cycles, and begin walking the path of ancient British shamanism.

Through Zenned Out, Cassie has self-published her best-selling *Goddess Discovery Book* and oracle card deck, *The Ritual Deck*. In 2020, she authored *The Zenned Out Guide to Understanding Auras*, *The Zenned Out Guide to Understanding Chakras*, *The Zenned Out Guide to Understanding Crystals*, and *The Zenned Out Guide to Understanding Tarot*. Learn more about Cassie and her other products at **ZennedOut.com** and visit her blog **ZennedOut.com/blog** for an abundance of free resources!

·•❂ REFERENCES ◁•·

Ahlquist, Diane. *Moon Spells: How to Use the Phases of the Moon to Get What You Want*. Avon, MA: Adams Media, 2002.

Alden, Temperance. *Year of the Witch: Connecting with Nature's Seasons Through Intuitive Magick*. Newburyport, MA: Weiser Books, 2020.

Billington, Penny. *The Path of Druidry: Walking the Ancient Green Way*. Woodbury, MN: Llewellyn Publications, 2020.

Chamberlain, Lisa. *Wicca Wheel of the Year Magic: A Beginner's Guide to the Sabbats, with History, Symbolism, Celebration Ideas, and Dedicated Sabbat Spells*. Chamberlain Publications, 2017.

Forest, Danu. *The Magical Year: Seasonal Celebrations to Honor Nature's Ever-Turning Wheel*. London: Watkins Media Limited, 2016.

Hall, Judy. *The Crystal Bible: A Definitive Guide to Crystals*. Blue Ash, OH: Walking Stick Press, 2003.

Kynes, Sandra. *Llewellyn's Complete Book of Correspondences: A Comprehensive & Cross-Referenced Resource for Pagans & Wiccans*. Woodbury, MN: Llewellyn Publications, 2013.

Lazic, Tiffany. *The Great Work. Self-Knowledge and Healing Through the Wheel of the Year*. Woodbury, MN: Llewellyn Publications, 2016.

Nock, Judy Ann. *The Modern Witchcraft Guide to the Wheel of the Year: From Samhain to Yule, Your Guide to the Wiccan Holidays*. Avon, MA: Adams Media, 2017.

Rajchel, Diana. *Samhain, Rituals, Recipes & Lore for Halloween: Llewellyn's Sabbat Essentials*. Woodbury, MN: Llewellyn Publications, 2016.

Van Der Hoeven, Joanna. *The Awen Alone: Walking the Path of the Solitary Druid. Pagan Portals*. Hants, UK: Moon Books, 2014.

Wallis, Faith. *Bede: The Reckoning of Time, Translated Texts*. Liverpool, UK: Liverpool University Press, 1999.

© 2021 by Quarto Publishing Group USA Inc.
Text and Illustrations © 2021 by Cassie Uhl

First published in 2021 by Rock Point,
an imprint of The Quarto Group,
142 West 36th Street, 4th Floor,
New York, NY 10018, USA
T (212) 779-4972 F (212) 779-6058
www.QuartoKnows.com

Rock Point titles are also available at discount for retail, wholesale, promotional, and bulk purchase. For details, contact the Special Sales Manager by email at specialsales@quarto.com or by mail at The Quarto Group, Attn: Special Sales Manager, 100 Cummings Center Suite 265D, Beverly, MA 01915 USA.

10 9 8 7 6 5 4 3 2 1

ISBN: 978-1-63106-774-7

Library of Congress Control Number: 2021938207

PUBLISHER: Rage Kindelsperger
CREATIVE DIRECTOR: Laura Drew
MANAGING EDITOR: Cara Donaldson
EDITOR: Keyla Pizarro-Hernández
COVER AND INTERIOR DESIGN: Sydney Martenis

Printed in China